≪EXPLAINING≫ ADOPTION

TO YOUR ADOPTED CHILD

This book is about explaining to your child
that he or she is adopted.
If you want to know more about adoption itself,
some of the books listed on page 30
might interest you.

Published by
British Agencies for Adoption & Fostering
11 Southwark Street
London SE1 1RQ
A company limited by guarantee
Registered London 1379092
Registered Charity 275689

© BAAF 1987
ISBN 0 903534 71 1

Designed by Andrew Haig
Illustrated by Geraldine Spence
Typeset by Intertype Ltd
Printed in England by Concise Print Ltd

Acknowledgements:

This book could not have been written without the
wholehearted collaboration of many people with
experience in adoption, in particular: Gill Pittman, Hilary
Chambers and Caroline Archer of PPIAS; Pam Hodgkins
of NORCAP; Hedi Argent of Parents for Children; the
staff of the Post-Adoption Centre; the many BAAF staff
who have contributed ideas and suggestions; Marian
Burch; Abigail Monkhouse.
BAAF is grateful to PPIAS and NORCAP for permission
to reprint quotations from their newsletters.

Some of the information in this book originally appeared
in the earlier BAAF publication *Explaining Adoption*, first
published in 1972 (most recent edition 1982).

CONTENTS

_W_ hether you have just become an adoptive parent or whether you have been one for years, you'll know that one of the most important things about adoption is that *your child understands about it*. If you are worried about explaining it to your child, we hope that this book – which has been based on the personal experiences of many adopted people and many adopters – will help to make it easier for you.

Nowadays all kinds of children are adopted, from newborn babies to toddlers, from older children to teenagers. Children from different cultures and from different countries. Children who never knew their 'birth' parents and children who have strong memories of them. Children who are healthy and children with handicaps, either mental or physical or both. Because children adopted as babies or toddlers are likely to need more explanation about adoption than

WHY TELLING YOUR CHILD IS SO IMPORTANT

those adopted at an older age, we have included information about 'telling' from the earliest age, although we realise this may not be appropriate for all readers. We hope that, whatever your circumstances, you will find some useful information here.

Why is 'telling' so vital?
Everyone has the *right* to know about their own history and most people, sooner or later, feel a deep *need* to know about it. What are their roots? Where did they get their physical characteristics – the colour of their hair, their height, their weight? People who live with their birth parents have all this history at their fingertips, and it's easy to take it all for granted. But those who are adopted also need to know these things: their adoptive parents provide them with loving care, take responsibility for them and make decisions for them, stand up for them and protect them, but they did not give them life, and adopted people have the right to know about this basic part of their history as well.

The strongest relationships are based on *truth* – adopters and adopted people have both realised this for many years, and laws have now been passed to support it, allowing adopted people to see their original birth certificates at the age of 17 or 18. So anyone who has not already been told can find out either then or later when they need their birth certificate (for example, to get a passport or to get married). In reality, of course, even if they are not told by their adopters, most children have found out long before this: perhaps from an overheard conversation between adults who know (relatives, teachers, doctors), or an accusation at school that they 'don't look like their parents', or the chance finding of a document at home, or – perhaps worst of all – from a thoughtless remark during a family row: 'Well, you certainly don't get it from *me*!'

Experiences like these can leave a lasting scar upon children and can damage their relationship with the adoptive parent – sometimes permanently. Children who discover unexpectedly that a loved parent is not, after all, a blood relation have their faith and trust in that parent shattered. The relationship will never be the same again. Whereas those children who have grown up secure in the knowledge that they are adopted, and know that they are loved and valued, have a relationship with their adopters built on honesty and trust.

What if I don't want to tell my child?

If you're worried about telling your child, and wish you could avoid it, think about the future. The fact is that *sooner or later your child is going to find out.* Adoption can't be kept a secret forever – there are too many people involved, too many unanswered questions, too many lies. Suppose your child finds out, in one of the many possible ways, that you have been living a lie for years – how do you think you will all feel? Wouldn't it be much better if it came from you, in a gentle loving way and with the opportunity for all the explanations you can include? Adopted people who were not told and who found out themselves have said 'It wasn't so much that I was adopted that shattered me – more the fact that my mum and dad had been deceiving me for years.' See the quotes from adopted children opposite.

What to call the birth parents

We have used the term 'birth parent' to describe the child's biological parent. What term you use is up to you: 'first' parent is one possibility, and can also be used to describe divorced parents of your children's friends, thus showing that plenty of other children have 'first' mums and dads. For very young children, 'tummy mummy' sums it up very well. Some adopters prefer to use first names: 'Well, you grew in Elizabeth's tummy and then you came to mummy and daddy.' For obvious reasons, the term 'real parent' to describe the birth parent is not a good choice, as it may make you appear less 'real'. (See also 'What is a parent?' on page 21.)

《 Like many adoptees, I found my adoption papers whilst looking in the 'deed box'; my birth mother's first name I never forgot, although every other detail became a blur. I knew I could not discuss this with my mother because it had always been a taboo subject, her answer was 'If you loved me you wouldn't ask'. I was 12 years old when I found the adoption papers, just after my father died. 》

《 I did not know I was adopted until at the age of 12 it could no longer be kept secret: during our first week at High School we were asked to bring along our birth certificates as proof of our ages. This request threw mother into a panic: she said she would have to try and find mine. Later the other girls took turns to trot to the front of the class to show their long pink certificates to the teacher. Come my turn and I made an excuse to leave the room and there in the corridor stood my parents earnestly talking to the headmistress. I remember feeling sick and I knew I was going to be expelled as I had not produced my birth certificate. The four of us stood like a tableau looking at one another. The headmistress said to my parents 'I think you should tell her as soon as possible.' Tell me what? I had to wait until I arrived home at 4.30pm, by which time I was trembling with apprehension and unable to eat any tea. Mother silently handed me a small, pink square. A birth certificate? Not mine, surely? The date of birth was mine, the surname was mine too, but who on earth was this female? An unmarried mother, unable to care for me, indeed had positively neglected me, gave birth to me. 》

《 I knew I was adopted from a very early age, and that it had been a private adoption arranged by my adoptive mother's GP, following the termination on medical grounds of her own pregnancy. When I was about nine, while searching through my parents' wardrobe for hidden Christmas presents, I came across a birth certificate giving my natural mother's name, my own name at birth and her address at the time of my birth, along with my certificate of entry in the Adopted Children's Register. I read my birth certificate but felt such guilt at finding it, instinctively knowing that my adoptive mother would not have wanted me to see it, so that I quickly put it back and never mentioned that I had found it. 》

*T*he first and most important thing to tell is simply the fact that your child is adopted. It's best to do this from the very start, in a very simple way if the child is very young, and giving more detail gradually as the child gets older. But don't feel that you have to stress adoption all the time. It should be just one among the many things your child is gradually taking in during childhood.

It's important to remember that although adopted children are 'different', they're not *that* different! There are thousands and thousands of adopted children in Britain today, just as there are thousands of only children and thousands of children whose parents are divorced (and who also have two sets of parents). If you keep dwelling on the fact that adoption is special and different, you may find your child expects special treatment – for example at school. This could cause problems for all of you.

WHAT TO TELL YOUR CHILD

If you simply talk about your child's adoption in a matter-of-fact, down-to-earth way, your child will accept it in the same way. On the other hand, if you think of it as something which is difficult and embarrassing to talk about, your child will feel the same. And don't forget, it's up to *you* to bring the subject up – don't wait for the child to do it. One boy said 'My adoptive parents have always been very open about everything connected with my adoption and were ready to answer any of my questions. I, sadly, have not always had the courage to ask all I would have liked to.' Don't leave your child in this boy's position: offer all the information your child can cope with, as his or her interest in their past grows.

What information have you got?
Nowadays adoption agencies are required by law to give you, the adopter, written information about your child's background. It's up to you, too, to *ask questions.* Find out as much as you can about your child's birth parents – their

6

Some questions you might ask the social worker

What day was my child born, and at what time?
Was it an easy or difficult birth?
How long did my child stay with the birth mother?
Where did my child go then? (as much detail as possible, according to the child's age)
Where did the birth parents' families come from?
Where were they both living when my child was born?
How old was the birth mother? (and father?)
What did they look like?
What were their likes and dislikes?
What were their hobbies?
What sort of schools did they go to?
How did they get about (car, bike etc)?
Does my child have any brothers or sisters?

You will be able to think of other questions.

family history, their jobs, their medical history, their physical characteristics. Knowledge about things like height and build will come in useful the day your child asks questions like 'How come I'm so tall/short/fat/thin?'. And you really need medical information to be able to answer questions like 'Any family history of asthma/eczema/heart disease?' at the doctor's. Your child may turn out to be particularly keen on music, or sport, or mathematics, and it'd be useful to be able to say 'Well, your mother/father was a musician/dancer/footballer/engineer etc'. Anything you can find out will be valuable, but you may find you have to keep asking. The social workers who've worked with your child's birth parent(s) could have information that may not seem important to them but could be *very* important to your child. If you've been lucky enough to meet your child's birth parent(s), you might be able to get mementos of the child's early life from them.

And, most important, *write down* anything you find out. You might think you'll remember, but you might not need some of this information for 10 or 15 years and your memory may not be so good then! When you do need it, you'll find that having all the details written down will be invaluable. And obviously you'll need to keep it all in a safe place.

If you adopted your child years ago, and are missing this sort of information, it's still worth getting back in touch with the adoption agency to try and find out more. Social workers, foster parents and children's home staff may all remember and have useful facts to give you. Keeping in touch with them occasionally is a good idea and makes it easier to get further information later on.

You, the adopter, have taken on the responsibilities, as well as the pleasures, of being a parent to your child. One of the responsibilities is to help your child grow to be an adult secure in as much knowledge as possible about his or past. This information is their right – and you are the best person to see that your child has it.

Some comments from adoptive parents are opposite.

Why was I adopted?
This is the question which, however many times you have explained it, is likely to be the starting point for any discussion you have with your child. The simple answer 'Your birth mother couldn't look after you and I (we) wanted a child badly and so we got you' will do for a start. But why the birth mother couldn't manage will need explaining, in more detail as the child gets older.

《 It's essential to be absolutely honest, you mustn't tell them anything that isn't true or leave out anything important. By the time our kids are grown up they will probably be able to see their own social services records and if they find out that we've been in any way untruthful they'll never trust us again. 》

《 It's been a gentle revealing of facts over the years, sometimes softening the truth but never avoiding it if it was necessary to answer the question. Our children trust us to tell them the truth as far as we are able or to try to find out the answer for them. 》

《 In our family when one of the children has said 'I wish I grew in your tummy, mum', I have said 'Well, I would have liked to grow babies in my tummy but if I had it wouldn't have been you and you would have been given to a different mummy and daddy, so I think it's better as it is'. 》

Documents you will find useful
Written information about your child (required by law)
Photographs of your child as a baby, a toddler, etc
Photographs of your child's birth family
Any other documents or mementos of the child's birth family such as a letter from the birth mother.
A life story book about your child, if one has been prepared (see also pages 12 and 13)

As already mentioned, the best way to approach telling your child about adoption is to take it for granted as something matter-of-fact from the start. So first you need to feel comfortable about being an *adoptive* parent. If you don't, then this an area which needs to be recognised and explored, perhaps with another adoptive parent. Your child will quickly sense it if you feel uncomfortable. Whereas if you feel good about it, you'll convey this to your child in many different ways. Your child will grow up in the knowledge that being adopted is a good thing, and that firm base will stand him or her in good stead as years go by. Whatever your child's age, warmth and affection are very important, and if you can build into your cuddles some endearments that include the word 'adopted' it will come to have a very positive meaning for your child.

WHEN TO TELL YOUR CHILD

When your child is a baby or toddler
If you adopted your child when he or she was very young, you can start your explaining at a very early age. The fact that your child is adopted will then just be another fact, to be taken in along with all the other facts being learnt. Your child won't understand what 'adoption' really means, but will become familiar with the term as something positive.

If you first meet your child at the toddler stage, it is even more important for you to cover this ground. Your child has already had some disturbing and unsettling experiences and you need to provide an explanation for these gently and gradually along with the security and warmth that will replace them. Of course very young children will not really understand what it's all about, and you will have to answer the same questions many times, but this doesn't matter. What matters is that you are building up an acceptance in your child of knowledge about his or her past and about you, and that you are doing it in a cheerful relaxed way.

When your child starts school
Your child may be at the age to start going out and about – to playgroup, nursery school or primary school, or just to play with other children. At this age children are beginning to explore the wider world around them, even though they still see themselves as the centre of the universe. They need to see where they fit into this world, and if they are adopted they need the words to explain to their friends about it. (You can read about what we call 'cover stories' on page 12.) At this age they'll be beginning to understand a bit more about what adoption means, so you need to raise the issue gently and reassuringly from time to time and be prepared to answer difficult questions.

From ages eight or nine onwards
At the age of eight or nine children start to think of their birth parents as real people, as personalities in their own right. Now, more than ever, it is important for you to feel comfortable with the circumstances of your child's background – to feel sympathy and concern for the predicament which faced your child's birth parents and to begin to explain this to your child. But don't criticise or complain about their behaviour: if children feel that their birth parents were 'bad' in any way, they sometimes assume that this means they are bad too, and that it's their own fault their parents couldn't keep them. You'll need to be careful with the explanations you use: if you say that the birth mother was too poor to keep your child, they may worry that you'd give them up if *you* fell on hard times; if you say that there was no father to help, they may ask why their friends with single parents haven't been given up for adoption too. You'll need to balance this with an acceptance that everything in the birth family was not rosy, and that adoption was for the best. And you can build in your thankfulness and pleasure that *you* were able to become your child's parent.

Adolescence
Perhaps the first and most comforting thing to remember about the adolescent child's problems is that *all parents have to face them*. Most young

people, whether adopted or not, go through a period of crisis during their teens, and there's not much you can do to avert this. Sometimes a person's curiosity about origins reaches a peak at the same time, making it all seem much worse. A strong relationship based on openness and trust will certainly help, though it may not feel like that at the time. It should help to go over all the old ground again about how each one of us is unique: we all have our basic inheritance, from the people who gave us life; we all have different life experiences, from where we live and the sort of families we grow up in; and we all have different chances to explore and use our talents and abilities. All these things – not just one of them – make us the people we are. Adolescents often find it easier to talk to someone other than a parent about things that matter most to them and if this is the case with your child, try not to feel hurt. You'll get through it – it just takes stamina! Try to keep remembering that you were the same once, and that you got over it. And remember that many of the doubts, difficulties and dilemmas which arise with adopted teenagers have nothing to do with adoption but are just part of growing up.

Your child's own story
Long before your child is old enough to go to school you will be faced with questions like 'Where did I come from?' All parents are. You can answer simple, direct questions like this with simple, direct answers like 'You grew in someone else's tummy and then you came to join our family'. You can build on this by reading from relevant picture books but, best of all, tell your child's *own* story, which will almost certainly become a great favourite. If you don't have a life story book for your child, start to put one together. The story of 'the day mummy (and daddy) got me' can be used to convey great excitement and pleasure and can be illustrated with any details possible – like the clothes you all wore, the way you travelled, what the weather was like and what everybody concerned said.

« We introduced things gradually to our daughter – the fact that her mother couldn't manage to look after her family of seven children satisfied her at first, but she soon wanted to know why she couldn't manage. This led to the fact that her father was away from home a lot so she had to cope alone. This again satisfied her for a while – she described her father as a 'wanderer' – but gradually she wanted to know why he was away so much and we had to tell her that he sometimes stole things and got sent to prison. We tried not to imply that he was a bad man but that he took drugs and needed money to buy them. She is now strongly anti-drugs but seems to feel that people who take them are 'silly' rather than 'bad'. »

« There's no question of sitting down and saying 'We've got something to tell you'. The situation is one which is lived out from day to day. The facts filter through gradually, some in answer to questions put usually when you're in the middle of trying to cross a busy road or writing 'Happy Birthday' on a cake, and some you produce yourself whenever the opportunity arises. »

« Our daughter, adopted as a baby, loves to hear her 'own' story over and over again with different details added at each telling. Long before she could talk or possibly understand the meaning of adoption she knew she was our 'darling adopted daughter', while her elder sister was our 'darling daughter'. She was, therefore, always aware of a difference but one that had no bearing on our love for both of them. Later, when she was able to ask about adoption it was possible to tell her simply and naturally that her sister grew in my tummy whereas she grew in Pauline's tummy. »

9

*I*f you have adopted a child (or children) and have not told them that they are adopted, the time has come for you to face this difficult moment. It's best if you think it through very carefully beforehand, and don't rush into things. Your child's age and stage of development will affect how you approach the subject, and how much you tell. If you have allowed your child to believe that you are his or her birth parent(s) you will have now to admit that you didn't feel able to tell the truth before and now you wish you had. Perhaps you thought you were protecting your child – then say so! Remember that your child needs to hear the truth from *you*, not from anyone else, if they are to trust you.

How best to get started depends on your circumstances, and you know your own child best. You need to try to find a way of bringing the subject up gently and naturally – perhaps in

IF IT'S DIFFICULT TO TELL

the light of some news story or the fact that a friend or relative is pregnant or is adopting. Perhaps you might start a discussion about where people you know were born, or you could start going through your photograph album and start talking about the day you brought your child home. However you decide to do it, find a time when your child is relaxed and not preoccupied with other matters that seem important, such as an end-of-term play or exams. Try to ensure that you and your child can talk together about the subject in privacy and without interruptions. Don't do it at a time when people will be calling round or the phone will be ringing. If you have built up a pleasant and loving atmosphere in which the child feels safe and secure, it will be easier.

Telling particularly distressing facts
There are some facts that will always be very difficult to face. Your child may be the result of an incestuous union, or of rape. Or possibly the necessity for adoption may have arisen because

one of the birth parents abused or rejected your child: they may even be in prison as a result. Tragic episodes do occur in the lives of some young children, and if this is true of your child it will be necessary to explain what happened – although exactly what you tell and how you tell it will vary as your child grows older and has more understanding of the world.

However difficult it may be, try not to judge your child's birth parents too harshly. If your child is the result of rape or incest, it helps if you can see these acts as a weakness rather than as criminality. Your child's parent needed help and didn't get it. Many 'sex offenders' are sad people who cannot control their instincts but regret them terribly afterwards, for as long as they live. The old saying 'Hate the sin, not the sinner' may help here. If your child was rejected as a baby because of some handicap (see also pages 18 and 19), or was abused before being taken away from his or her parents, try to put yourself in their place. Their circumstances may have been impossible for them to cope with. Try to imagine how you would feel if you had never had a loving relationship with anyone or if you were faced with a combination of poverty, loneliness, unemployment, inadequate housing and so on: you too might be driven to breaking point. Of course, it's one thing to accept terrible facts as a mature adult, but much more difficult to convey them to a child in an acceptable way. But however inadequate you feel your child's parents may have been, there are always good points: try to find these out and emphasise them to your child. Talk about the parents in simple language the child can understand, and be sure it has the ring of compassion: if the child feels that you understand and can accept the facts, it will be that much easier for the child to accept them too and forgive the parents. One adopter told us, 'Children can accept anything if you tell them in the right way; it's the grown ups who find things difficult to accept.'

If, however, you feel that the problem is just too big for you to handle, you might find it helpful to talk it over with another parent who's been in a similar position. Contact the adoptive parents' organisation PPIAS (see page 28), as it's very likely that they can help. If you'd like help from a trained counsellor, the Post Adoption Centre (page 29) will provide a sympathetic ear and the benefit of much experience. Other telephone advice services are listed on page 29. Or you could contact the adoption agency which placed your child with you.

If your child's adoption was contested

Your child's birth parent(s) may have wanted to keep the child, but for many different reasons may not have been allowed to. Perhaps your child had been living with you long enough to have formed a close bond which it would have been damaging to break; or perhaps the birth parents were considered unable to bring up a child adequately. Whatever the reason, you have a delicate task ahead. While your child should not run the risk of feeling rejected like many adopted children do, he or she may go through a phase of feeling that the birth parents were treated unfairly – by you as well as by the state. Your best bet is to keep showing your love for your child and your sympathy for the birth parents' predicament, while accepting the fact that what was done was for the best.

《 We had to help Joanna cope with the fact that her father had sexually abused her. We started to talk about different kinds of love, about the way mummies and daddies love each other being different from the way children love parents and parents love children. We explained that some grown-ups get things muddled up and don't have the same rules as other people. We said 'When your daddy was young his daddy loved him in the way that mummies and daddies love each other so he thought it was okay to love you like that. But that is wrong and I know it's wrong and you knew it was wrong and that's why you told your teacher'. 》

《 You need to start as early as possible – by the time John (who had been battered as a baby) was two-and-a-half he knew who had hit him and where the bruises were and who'd seen them and that was why he was taken away. We said 'Well, when you were only three weeks old you used to cry a lot and your first mummy and daddy thought you were being naughty and they smacked you hard, hard enough to make very big bruises and then the nurse came and saw them and thought they shouldn't smack such a little baby so you were taken away and given to parents who wouldn't smack you. Your first mummy and daddy were very young and they didn't know that little babies aren't being naughty when they cry but cry because they're hungry and want to be cuddled'. 》

11

Children who remain with their birth families throughout childhood have many ways of knowing about their past. Their parents and relatives – including older brothers or sisters – have memories and stories to tell. During childhood some of these stories become part of the family history, to be brought up and laughed about or wondered over again and again. Often there are photograph albums or collections of slides (even, today, video-tapes) of the child at different stages of growing up. Most people know if they were born in hospital, at a nursing home or at home, and many know the time of birth and who else was involved – for example, if a friend or relative helped look after any other children in the family at the time. As the children grow up, other events – moving house, going to nursery school, accidents, illnesses, friendships and family celebrations like birthdays and weddings – all become part of the family folk-lore of shared experiences.

For children separated from their birth parents, it's different. They have no family 'keepers of their personal history'. They have to rely on outsiders – social workers, staff at children's homes and hospitals, medical records. For these children – like your adopted child – their past is often a mystery, or a jumbled collection of memories that no one can ever precisely put into place. Luckily, social workers and others involved have begun to realise that helping children understand what went on in their early lives and coming to terms with it is the best way to enable them to move forward into the present and future. Depending on the age of your child and the circumstances, you may already have a *life story book* for your child. If you haven't, think about starting one.

See what you already have that could form part of your child's 'personal history book'.

HELPING YOUR CHILD TO REMEMBER

'Cover stories'

When your child makes new friends or meets new people (like teachers), they'll ask questions. It's vital that your child has answers ready and doesn't start making things up – which are so difficult to put right later. Make sure that your child has an explanation ready for the things that may seem odd to an outsider. Being adopted is not something to be ashamed of, but it is something that needs explaining. One mother told us 'My daughter came home from school upset. A child had told her that adoption means that her mum had given her away and had never loved her. She was very hurt and bewildered. She was anxious to hear again how she was adopted – that her mum had loved her so much and had wanted only the best for her but was worried that she could not provide this.' Help your child to be prepared for this kind of thing, and ready with answers – answers which are the truth, if not the whole truth.

Photographs, letters, cards and any other documents are a good start. But if your child joined you past babyhood, most of all you need to depend on your child's memory and on the contacts you have who can help you – workers at the adoption agency who placed your child with you, in particular. (See also pages 6 and 7 for information you might be able to get hold of.) Using a loose-leaf folder means that as more details emerge they can be added in. It also enables the child to remove any particularly private bits before showing the book to friends or relatives, if they want to.

Remember that this may not be an easy exercise. Your child may not want to remember some of his or her early experiences, but to make a life story book all known facts should be included. You would be well advised to talk to the social worker who worked with your child before you start. Your child may get angry during the time you're working on the book and may take it out on you, the old hurt and bewilderment coming back. But you are undoubtedly the best person to do this work – you know your child better than anyone else does now, and you have the opportunities that no one else has. You can choose the times when your child is in the right mood to do this kind of thing. You can continue for as short or as long a time as you want. And, because you are now your child's family, you can do this task from a safe, secure base. You can use these times with your child for building on the warm loving relationship of the present. And as the book comes up to date, you can start adding the *memories of the present* to those of the past.

Making life story books

If you decide to make a life story book with your child, you could invest in another BAAF book which goes into the subject in much greater detail. *Making life story books* by Tony Ryan and Rodger Walker includes lots of suggestions for clarifying your child's past – making maps of the local area with moves marked, playing with dolls and models to indicate family members, drawing up family trees and much more. An example from the book is shown here.

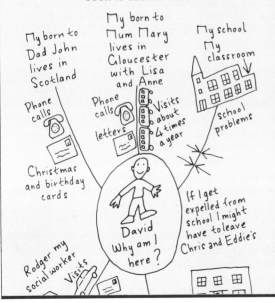

《 A significant event came when we were writing my daughter's life story: she wrote: 'I always thought it was my fault I was taken away' – something she had never voiced but felt able to write and subsequently to talk about. She was then able to accept that circumstances beyond her control, and beyond the control of her parents, had caused it all to happen. Harder things to face such as sexual abuse have also been best dealt with initially through the medium of the life story book leading to discussions on a personal level: the action of writing unpleasant things allowing a more detached way in. She has even said, 'Oh dear – I knew I would have to write this awful part one day'. But she has faced up to it and seems relieved to have done so. When I suggested that some day she might want to destroy the unpleasant parts of her book she said 'Oh no – I couldn't do that, it's part of my life'. So now when she wants to share her book with someone the offending pages are temporarily removed and only left in for a handful of very trusted people. 》

《 Our daughter, adopted as a seven year old, shies away from asking personal questions or referring to her life before she joined our family, and very often we have to look for opportunities to refer to her first six years. Because this was a time when she did not have a normal family life, she is often too anxious to blot out and forget these years. In an effort to help her sort out her very muddled memories and to fill in the gaps, we started to make a scrapbook. It took a good deal of persistence to get any relevant information from the social services department, and eventually I sent the social worker a long list of questions saying I would be grateful if only a few of them could be answered. I knew it was possible for him to visit her biological mother as she had been contacted in order to sign the consent form. I included all sorts of questions in the hope of gleaning information about her early babyhood and, considering the passage of time, I was grateful for the answers I received. We then started slowly over many months to build her scrapbook. As writing was then a considerable labour for her I did most of the simple factual writing leaving her to put in the important information such as the date of her birth, where she was born, her first name etc. We were able to illustrate the book with pictures and maps of the place of her birth, and we were fortunate in being able to obtain some photographs through various social workers and house-parents. Working on the book has given us both a wonderful opportunity to deepen our relationship in discussing a very intimate part of herself. 》

*I*f your child is of a different race to you, then you have an additional responsibility and some extra explaining to do. The chances are that you are white and your child is black or of 'mixed parentage' and these pages have been written on the basis of this assumption. Much of the information on pages 16 and 17 probably also applies to you.

Like all adopted children, your child has already lost his or her birth parents: it's up to you to ensure that all that went with those parents isn't lost too. Your child needs to know all about his or her background, race and culture – and this means that *you* need to know about these things. Of course, like all adopters you need as much information as you can get about your child's birth parents, as described on pages 6 and 7. But you need much more than this. In today's society, people from minority groups – black people in particular – are often portrayed

What else can you do?

Every day, your child hears the word 'black' used to mean 'wrong' and the word 'white' to mean 'right'. Think of 'getting a black mark', 'blacklisted', 'in a black mood', 'blackmail', 'black market', and so on. All these terms have a negative meaning. Where does this leave your black child? No wonder the phrase 'black is beautiful' was coined: black people need to believe in themselves, just like everyone else does. At least in your family and social circle, you can try to avoid using words in this way. Try to put yourself in your child's place, and be sensitive to their feelings. If you go on using 'black' to mean something bad, you too are helping to give your child a poor impression of their colour and themselves.

IF YOUR CHILD IS OF A DIFFERENT RACE

by newspapers and television in a very negative way, or ignored altogether. How often does your child see black people featured in TV advertisements, for example? How many characters in comics are black? How many books about black children has your child read? The answer to all these questions is probably 'Not many'. And even when black people *are* portrayed in the media, it's often only in connection with 'inner city crime' or perhaps as the 'loony Left'. Yet the vast majority of black people in this country, just like the vast majority of white people, are law-abiding middle-of-the-road folk, going about their daily business in the same way as anyone else. So it's up to you to set the record straight. You have to challenge these stereotypes your child faces every day and in many subtle forms. So first of all it's vital that *you* have a positive attitude towards your child's race.

The best way to approach this, if you haven't already, is to make some friends from the same race as your child. Not only will you be able to find out much more about your child's racial heritage, but you will also be giving them a positive picture – adults of their own race to look up to. The black child in a white family is not only a minority in society but in their own family too. How much more important, then, is it for you to help your child in any way you can to cope with what the rest of society is presenting them with. To do this you need the support of black people who share the experience and so understand better than you do what your child has to face.

As well as the many subtle ways your child is told that black is less valuable than white, there is also open racism – and children can be faced with this from a very early age. Racial abuse is different from any other kind of insult. Imagine being called a 'white bastard' or 'whitey' as if the word 'white' were an insult in itself – it's difficult, isn't it? Yet black children have grown used to this. Sooner or later your child will face racism and racist insults: will they come to you for help? Or will they see you on the same side as those who've insulted them, because of your colour? *Colour cannot be ignored.* At the earliest age, your child needs to be aware that there are people of different colours in the world and that no one colour is better than another. If you have built up a warm understanding relationship with your child based on open discussion about race and colour, and have included in your circle of friends people from other races, your child will recognise that although much of society may hold racist views, at least you don't. Your chances then of maintaining a good relationship with your child, and of supporting them when they come up against racism, right through the adolescent years and into adulthood, are that much better.

« *Possibly the most vital thing of all is to try and stay in touch with our children, to talk with them, to learn from them. You may not face the frequent put-downs and slights – or worse – that they do, but you can share their humiliations and embarrassments, and discuss with them ways of dealing with racism – when to confront people, when to walk away with dignity. You can play your part too by refusing to watch unacceptable programmes on TV, and by openly expressing your disgust over racist comment and action expressed in the media or by people you meet. These skills can be learned too – from your black friends.* »

Where can you get more help?

A very useful source of help for families like yours is a pack produced by PPIAS. Called *Information and resources for mixed race families,* it includes lists of ways of getting to know people, where to go on family outings, where to buy toys, games, books, etc. It ends with a list of publications about tackling racism.

BAAF has also produced a *Black issues resource list* which is available free on request. You may also like to encourage your child's school to use some excellent materials from the Afro-Caribbean Education Resource Project (ACER), Wyvil School, Wyvil Road, London SW8 2TJ. Called *Ourselves,* they are aimed at middle-school pupils and concentrate on self-image and identity. ACER are also producing a series of books for younger children called 'I'm special'. The first four books are *Me, My Body, My Senses* and *My Feelings.*

Also useful are two little books for black children in a series called 'Black like me'. The first one, *Black identity,* aims to encourage a positive self-image and the second, *Black pioneers,* describes the work of black inventors, scientists, doctors and civil rights campaigners. Available from the National Children's Bureau, 8 Wakley Street, London EC1V 7QE.

« *I also remember trying to talk to people about my origins and would ask questions like 'why am I black?', 'where did my real father come from?'. The answers I would receive would be along the lines of 'it's nothing to worry about, you are British' or 'England is your home, you are one of us'. These answers may well have been well-meaning, but when I was older I was bitter about them. My strong advice to white families offering homes to black children is to be honest with them when they want to talk about such sensitive issues. Don't be afraid to discuss with them their origins or the harsh realities of the world outside. If need be, get support from relations or friends or people from outside the immediate family rather than shy away from the subject. It may well be that such discussions will cause stress or hurt to your child at times, but warmth, love and honesty and really sharing sensitive issues will overcome stress or hurt. The benefits that will be given are that your child will grow and develop, and will very likely be a more well adjusted person who is able to face the realities of what life can be like without the protection of the family.* »

*T*oday there are an increasing number of children in Britain who have been adopted from abroad. If you are the parent of such a child, you have the responsibility of explaining to your child not only about their adoption but also about their country. And it's not an easy matter: how to present your child's country in a positive manner when you may feel that one of your reasons for adopting your child was to give them a better life than they could hope for there. But it is in your own interests, as well as your child's, that you do so – or you run the risk of being alienated from them later on. Just as so many children adopted in Britain feel the need to find out about their origins at some point in their lives, so children from other countries also have a need (and a right) to their own cultural heritage.

You and your child may have disadvantages in addition to those described for transracial

2 Subscribe to local magazines and newspapers. Public libraries have international press directories to help you locate them. Keep the back issues for school projects later on. And check *Keesing's Record of World Events* at your library. It is very international, up to date, excellently indexed, and has been going for many years. It concentrates on politics. Photocopy and keep the relevant pages.

3 Learn the local language. You should be able to pronounce names correctly and be able to transliterate the writing system. Even if you never learn to read them, buy some books in the local language. You may be able to exchange board and room for language lessons from foreign students.

4 Get a pen friend, for you now, for your child later. There are international associations to help you find one, or you could advertise locally.

IF YOUR CHILD IS FROM A DIFFERENT COUNTRY

adopters on pages 14 and 15. You may have very little information about your child's birth parents. Your child's life story book may have to start with your arrival in their life. Any additional information you can glean from your contact in the original country will be vitally important to your child. And, as indicated on these pages, links with the country of origin can be built up, however slim they may seem to begin with.

Your child's ethnic identity

Here is a list of suggestions of ways to build up your child's ethnic identity. It is useful for any child adopted from abroad, as well as for black British children whose ancestors came from the Caribbean, Africa, India, etc. The term 'local' applies to the child's original country.

1 Give your child an appropriate name. Try to find a name which is distinctive but still easily pronounced. Sources: books, diplomats, foreign students, aid workers, linguists and anthropologists specialising in the region.

5 Sponsor a child from the area through Action Aid or a similar organisation, and keep all the material you receive.

6 Collect things: stamps, money, arts and crafts, tapes and records, musical instruments, clothes, games, dolls, etc. Sources: stamp and coin dealers, Oxfam and other aid organisations' catalogues, etc.

7 Go to sports events where local touring sides are playing. Learn distinctive local games and sports (anthropology texts can help here).

8 Learn to cook local foods and go to national restaurants if you get the chance.

9 Find out about local holidays and observe them in your home. Learn about local religions.

10 Go to museums and art galleries. The Museum of Mankind in London is excellent. Watch out for travelling exhibitions or special events at the Commonwealth Institute, embassies and museums. Don't forget their book and gift shops.

11 Make a point of seeing films (travel and features) about or shot in the country.

12 If you hear of people who have been to the area and know it well, cultivate them. If you hear of someone who is going there, impose on them: get them to take pictures (provide the film), buy books, records, artefacts, clothes, toys, stamps, foods, etc. Sources: mission boards, British Council, IVS, VSO, etc.

13 If you can, listen to local radio broadcasts on their external services. For wavelengths and transmission times use the *World Television and Radio Handbook*, or contact the BBC World Service.

14 Some foreign broadcasting services have tapes of radio and TV programmes for sale, including those to accompany language courses, which can help you with number 3 above.

15 Join interracial groups here, and their equivalents in the local country.

16 Other societies to consider: regional-interest and anthropological, zoological, linguistics, geographical societies; expatriate societies (of locals here); local chamber of commerce or friendship societies. Any of these might provide contacts, including people from that area living near you that you didn't know about, and they may be sources of cheap flights or package tours.

17 Travel: extremely important if you can afford it. A package tour for two weeks is better than nothing but the more frequent, for longer periods, away from the tourist traps, the better.

18 Consider sending your child to school in his or her local area staying with a local family. Much depends on your contacts, the local language of instruction, the curriculum, etc, but a 'lost year' in examination terms here may be more than compensated for by the benefits in identity formation. Financial problems might be eased by an exchange, saving living expenses if nothing else, and giving you a temporary live-in resource.

19 Check travel agencies, national airlines and train companies and tourist bureaux for brochures and posters.

20 Get books, magazines, tapes and records. Try third-world and black bookshops and specialised shops for expatriates in Britain (including grocery shops). You may also be able to order direct from shops in the local country: if you do, enclose international reply coupons (get them at the Post Office) to pay the return postage, or you may not get an answer.

21 Use your local library. Librarians can often turn up information in unlikely places.

22 Check second-hand bookshops, junk and charity shops, and jumble sales and auctions. It is a good idea for you to read everything first, to vet it for unconscious ethnocentrism or racism, before letting your child or anyone else have it.

23 Check up on your child's legal status. Some rights (residence, citizenship) may be unaffected by place of birth or subsequent nationality or adoptive status. They may depend solely on ethnic status. Unless there is a real need, don't discard your child's original citizenship.

BAAF is grateful to Roger Fenton and PPIAS for permission to include this list, which first appeared in a much longer form in the Summer 1987 edition of the PPIAS newsletter (number 46).

《 *So the day of the court hearing came. I told Shanti afterwards that the nice man who had smiled at her (the judge!) had said that she could really and truly be our little girl for ever. Of course she doesn't remember this, but from then on, all we did was to answer all her questions as truthfully as we could. Often she would ask, 'Didn't my mother love me?' and I always said, 'Yes, she did. She couldn't keep you because there was no daddy and no money and she wanted you to have a daddy, a mummy and brothers and sisters.' (We have three older children born to us.) The first day she was at school, as she ran out calling, 'Mummy!' another child said, 'That's not your real Mummy!' My heart sank for her, but she said, 'Yes she is! She's not my first Mummy, but she's my real Mummy.' Now that was entirely her own choice of words.* 》

*I*f you have adopted a child with a disability, your task will be different from that of other adopters. Of course your child still has a right to know about their origins, just as any child does, and of course the dangers of your child finding out about their adoption accidentally are just as serious as for any adopted child. Indeed, because your child probably feels 'different' and perhaps 'second best', finding out that they are different in yet another way – by being adopted – can be particularly devastating. Not only are they handicapped, they may feel that they have also been rejected by their birth parents. Yet you have a strength to offer your child: you really did *choose* him or her, handicap and all. And in a world where handicap usually means 'disadvantage', this is a very strong point. Telling your child that he or she was chosen by you will give you both a warm feeling and may make up

IF YOUR CHILD IS DISABLED

to your child for some of their feelings of difference.

Your child's birth parents, too, are probably different – they may be a securely settled married couple with other healthy children. The explanations you give your child, therefore, have to stress the positive side of things. Whatever their views at the time, the birth parents probably gave up their child because they wanted the best for him or her. You, the adopters, were able to offer this 'best' – perhaps you have much more experience of looking after a person with a handicap, or have access to specialised leisure facilities or live near the hospital or school. Whatever the reason, you are the best family for your child.

If your child has a mental handicap
The fact that your child has a mental handicap doesn't mean they lose the right to know about and understand their own life story. Indeed, the distress and confusion your child could feel on finding out about their adoption unexpectedly

could, because of their more limited understanding, make this an even more threatening experience than usual. So it's up to you to find ways of explaining things at your child's own level. It will probably take longer for them to understand each point, so they probably need to start meeting these experiences sooner rather than later than other children. As their parents, you will know best when they are ready to approach the different aspects of their past, and how long it will take for them to comprehend each new experience. And just as you are developing their potential in other ways, so you can help them to understand their early experiences too. If you feel that you need expert help in this difficult field, contact one of the organisations listed on pages 28 and 29.

However profound your child's handicap, and however limited their understanding may seem, it's still worth going through the explaining process with them. They will understand that now they have consistent loving care from the same person (or people), and that's the most important thing.

Your child's story

Stories for young children are always a good way of telling them new things. On pages 30 to 32 we have listed some suggestions of basic illustrated books you might find helpful in explaining things to your child. And, just like any other child, yours will be fascinated by a story about themselves. All the details about being a baby, leaving the hospital, and the gradual process of growing up, illustrated with photographs and documents, will delight your child. (More about life story books is on pages 12 and 13.) Of course you will have to move at your child's pace – but all parents have to do this. And you will probably have to repeat the same points over and over – but this too is very common. You may have to work hard to make them realise the 'story' is about them, but it will be worth it. Some parents have found that a tape of the child's own story, which they can listen to over and over again, is a very useful way of explaining. You will know best how simple to keep your child's story, because you know your child best.

'Who is my real mummy?'

It might help, if your child says things like 'But who is my real mummy?', to ask simple questions like: Who puts you to bed? Who takes you to school? Who reads you stories? Who do you feel is your real mummy? Who do you want when you wake up in the night? Who do you think loves you more than anyone else in the world? Of course, you want them to understand about their birth mother too: if you approach it gently, you'll probably find that your child can cope with the idea of two mothers, 'real' in different ways.

《 One area of potential difficulty with a severely handicapped child like David is finding ways to help him build a positive self-image. As he struggles against frustration and a growing awareness of his difficulties and limitations, emphasis needs to be placed on those aspects of his life that he can develop and control – for example, personal relationships, intellectual skills, social contacts. An adopted or fostered child may also have to cope with the knowledge that he has already been rejected because of his handicaps and David often seeks reassurance that I knew he couldn't walk and still wanted him. It is painful to answer his many questions about why he can't walk or write or draw, but I have always answered truthfully but simply, and it does seem to help him to verbalise his feelings about his handicaps. 》

《 Like many adoptive parents of older, disturbed and handicapped children, we are sometimes told how 'brave' we are. Yet surely it is the children themselves who are so brave? To enter an alien household filled with strangers, when you hardly even know who you are yourself, is to show great courage. 》

《 I wrote down a little story for my daughter which I called 'Emma is adopted'. It's very easy, with a sentence or two on each page, and photographs of her and us. It tells the story of how she came to us in a very simple way, with lots of repeated bits. She's always loved it – at one time we used to have to read it to her half a dozen times a day. Now she's taken it all in, but she still goes back to it sometimes and we build on it and add pages. I can't think of a better way. 》

《 We met Kevin. We couldn't believe our emotions that day. We liked him, he appeared to like us. Perhaps the mental handicap wasn't as bad as we had thought. We returned a week later, and on this second meeting, the fact he was mentally handicapped had flown out of the window for us. We were too busy getting to know our son and making arrangements for him to come home. The joys he brought with him are unbelievable. We have never regretted that decision to go and visit the little boy we thought we couldn't cope with. Now, we cannot imagine nor want a life without him! Each milestone he reaches brings us the greatest of joys. The tears I shed before Kevin arrived were for sorrow and sadness. Since his arrival the tears have been of laughter and pure joy. 》

If you are a step-parent who has adopted – or who is thinking of adopting – your step-children, most of what appears elsewhere in this book will also be relevant to you and your step-children. Step-families are on the increase as the rate of divorce continues to be high, but adoption by step-parents has decreased. Because adoption cuts off legal ties with one birth parent, other arrangements – like varying the custody order, for example – are now seen as more appropriate, particularly where the child has strong links with the absent parent (who we've called the 'other birth parent' in this section).

But many step-parents *have* adopted their step-children and in some cases, where the children were young enough not to realise, have kept this information from the child. In the past, social workers weren't necessarily involved in step-parent adoptions, so it may have seemed easier to keep this secret. But when a step-parent

IF YOU ARE A STEP-PARENT

adopts, the parent with custody (the step-parent's partner) has to adopt too – usually this means the mother and the step-father together adopting the children – so the child has an *adoption certificate*, not a birth certificate. And at the age of 17 or 18, the child can see the original birth certificate. So all the same issues arise.

Adopting older children

For older children, where secrecy is not a possibility, other problems may appear. In cases of divorce, for example, the child may deeply resent the loss of the other birth parent – after all, divorce wasn't the child's idea and neither was the step-parent. The special relationship a child often has with a single parent is also put at risk by a step-parent. And the child may worry that if they start to love their new step-parent, they'll somehow risk losing their other birth parent's love. These issues, which arise in many step-families, can seem to be made more significant by adoption. It may make the child seem more secure – or it may increase their

feeling of loss about the other birth parent.

Whatever the situation, the child needs to be consulted and listened to and, if their wishes have to be over-ridden, helped to understand and to accept it. It hurts to lose a parent – you have to help the child understand that the other birth parent *isn't* lost. It's confusing to have three parents – two of the same sex: which one is 'Daddy'? Of course, not all children adopted by their step-fathers ever knew their birth fathers. But where the birth father is known – especially if he still keeps in contact with the child – it's up to you to make things clear. Life story books, as described on pages 12 and 13, can work wonders here, with family trees showing where everyone fits in. And some of the children's books listed on pages 30 to 32 may also come in useful in the explaining process. It's hard work, but so are most relationships that are worth having.

What is a parent?

To help a child understand, it might be useful to explain something about what being a parent means:

First and foremost, it means giving you *life* (your inheritance):
this includes the way you look
the way your brain and body works
some of the things you are good at
and like to do
some of the things you find difficult
and don't like

second, it means caring for you and bringing you up:
loving you and minding what happens to you
encouraging you and comforting you
looking after you physically
teaching you all the things you need to know
until you're independent

third, it means taking responsibility for you:
making important decisions about things like
schooling and future plans
providing for you in material ways
representing your needs until you're old
enough to do this yourself

A child needs all these things – and for most children, they all come from the birth parents. But for adopted children – including those adopted by step-parents – where the birth parent(s) aren't in a position to take on the second and third areas, it means having two sets of parents.

If you're thinking about adoption

We at BAAF have produced two leaflets about *step-parents and adoption*, one for England and Wales, one for Scotland. Both spell out the advantages and disadvantages of adoption for step-parents and tell you where to get more information. They are available direct from BAAF.

《 *Explaining it all to the children was the difficult bit. That they'd still be loved by their father and they should still love him – he'd still be their father. The fact that I'd be married to someone else didn't mean that they couldn't still see him. Then there were all the questions about what to call my second husband – and who to make cards for on Father's Day. We got round that one by getting them to make two each, and I think they ended up being quite proud of the fact – it put them one up on the others in their class.* 》

《 *We thought adopting the children would make us into a 'real' family – Colin would be much more their father than before. But actually it caused some problems – the kids didn't want him to order them about, and he felt that with the added responsibility, he could. It took ages before they accepted him and even now there are some arguments about it.* 》

《 *I was nine when my parents divorced and mum remarried when I was 11. At first I got on really well with my step-father and wanted him to adopt me, because we lost touch with my real father really quickly. But when I was a teenager it was nothing but rows, over everything I did. Then I wished he hadn't adopted me! But we're okay now.* 》

《 *I wasn't at all sure about the adoption idea. Lloyd wanted to adopt the girls and while it seemed a good idea for him I didn't like the idea of having to adopt them myself too. I mean, they were my kids! Then their father, Walter, wasn't too keen on it and that made the kids worried. They couldn't really understand it at all, and it seemed complicated enough without adding to it. So we decided against it in the end.* 》

《 When I first came to this family I was very frightened, because I had been moved from different homes before — they had been horrid. So I thought that because the other homes were not very nice to me that this family was going to be horrid. The first night I came I was not used to so many people around the house, and I was very confused, but soon – after about four weeks – I got used to my surroundings. Sometimes when social workers came I ran away into my bedroom because I thought that each time I would be taken away. I had used to always think about the past. But my foster parents taught me to look into the future, and what I would do and not what I had done. 》

《 The fact that I was not born to my parents has never, ever worried or saddened me; with loving and caring parents as I am lucky enough to have, whether or not we are related by blood does not matter to any of us. I feel that my sister and I belong as much to our parents as any of my friends do to their 'natural parents'. My reaction, when asked what I feel about my other family in another country is that I don't have another family: I've only ever known one mother, one father and one sister. We are all able to talk very freely about my sister's and my first families but they seem so distant, hardly connected with us at all. It seems slightly unreal to me. Maybe I should feel closer to my first parents. I don't know. After all, it was thanks to them that I am part of a very close family now. I hope they don't miss me; I hope they are able to speak about me as I am able to speak about them. Although I was born to them and I knew them for nine months I feel it's not so much who you're born to, it's who you spend your life with that matters. 》

《 I like living with my mummy and daddy and little sister. I grew in Maureen's tummy. I went to hospital to be born but then I had to live with somebody else. I was very sad but I loved my new parents. They loved me. I was adopted by my mummy and daddy. We went to Court to see if I could live with them. The judge said yes. I grew up to be a big girl and now I am six. I wanted a little sister so mummy and daddy said I could. Once again we went to Court to see if my little sister could live with us. The judge said yes. My sister is two now two and I like playing with her. 》

HOW ADOPTED

❮ Whenever my parents told me off or wanted me to do something I didn't want to do, I'd say 'My real mum would have let me' or 'She'd have understood'. I didn't mean it – I'd no idea whether she would or not – but it was a way of getting back at them. Somehow they put up with me even when I was trying to be so awkward like this. I even ran away twice but I went back. Later, when I met my first mother, I felt I had much more in common with them than with her after all. I didn't realise till years later how much this much have hurt them. ❯

❮ I can think back to situations when, as a child, people were trying to protect me from some harsh realities that I had to face eventually as an adult anyway. If these people had been less protective and willing to talk, I think that I might have been better able to deal with some of the stressful situations I had to face as a young adult. When I had problems with people, and I honestly knew that those problems arose because I was black, people looking after me would say 'just ignore them, they are only ignorant and did not know me' rather than helping me to cope by talking such issues through with me in order to better help me understand ❯

CHILDREN FEEL

❮ A question commonly asked of adopted people is 'How did you feel when you found out you were adopted?' It is a question I cannot answer. I never 'found out' I was adopted, it was just a fact I had known all my life. I must have been told of my adoption by the time I was three years old, and simply grew up with the knowledge. I was greatly loved, wanted and, as I was keen to tell playground adversaries, chosen. I was told I was adopted as the lady I was born to was unable to look after me. As only illness ever prevented mummy from looking after me, I assumed my natural mother had been ill. I equated illness with old age, and throughout my childhood visualised Rose, my natural mother, as a small, bent, old lady in a grey coat and felt hat. ❯

❮ I wanted to be adopted when I understood what it meant. I did so want to be part of a family and stay for good. I began to get very ill because I wanted to be adopted. When I was adopted I cried with happiness. Now I have been adopted I feel safe. I can stay with my family for as long as I please and that will be for as long as I live. I love my family very much. ❯

As has been pointed out already in this book, it's important not to see birth parents as inadequate or irresponsible. It's often difficult not to judge people, but you may not know all the circumstances. As you can imagine, mothers (and fathers) who give up their children don't, by and large, do it easily! There is usually a lot of heartache and emotional turmoil involved. If your child came to you as a baby, you may like to read some of the quotations from young mothers on the page opposite. If your child was older, as is more and more the case these days, think of the circumstances and try to put yourself in the birth parent's place. Remember that they will certainly feel a deep sense of regret and guilt at having given up a child. Almost always, they made their decision because they believed that it was the best for their child and was the most responsible thing they could do in the circumstances.

HOW BIRTH PARENTS FEEL

As the years go by, if there is no contact between the birth parents and the adopted child, many birth parents feel an overwhelming sense of loss, particularly around the date of the child's birth. As the time of the seventeenth or eighteenth birthday approaches, many anticipate the phone call or letter that means their child wants to make contact. If nothing happens they are kept in a state of uncertainty which is never far from the surface, though it may last years (even a lifetime).

Some parents, of course, feel differently. They may be in the position of having married and had other children and may never even have admitted to their partner that there was a previous child. They may feel dread at the thought of the 'knock on the door'. (Just as openness about adoption is the best thing, so openness about one's past is often the only way to real peace of mind in these circumstances.)

Explaining adoption to the birth parent's children

Many mothers whose children have been adopted of course go on to have other children. They then have to decide whether or not to tell *these* children about their earlier child. In this situation, as in the others described in this book, honesty is usually the best policy. Whether or not these children have the *right* to know that they have another brother or sister is an interesting question. But if the adopted child decides to look for their birth family, they and the rest of the family are likely to find out about it anyway. However, mothers in this position often find it very difficult to tell their children. They may worry that the children would be afraid of being given up too (depending on their age), or on how it would make them appear – callous, hard-hearted, promiscuous perhaps. It can be very difficult for young people today, growing up surrounded by single-parent families, to understand how different the world once was and what a stigma was attached to 'illegitimacy'. Nonetheless, the truth is still the best answer, with whatever detail the child can cope with at their age.

'Can I trace my child?'

As the law stands at present in Britain, adopted *children* can see their birth certificates at 17 or 18 and can, if they wish, try to trace their birth parents. But there is not usually much hope for birth parents who want to trace their children. Many parents, anxious to find out how their child fared, have been dismayed to discover that whatever they do it's unlikely that their child will ever find out that they were trying to make contact. Several organisations such as NORCAP and PAC (see pages 28 & 29) are pressing for a *national contact register* which will enable this sort of information to be kept available for the child should they ever want it. You can find out more about the current situation by getting in touch with one of these organisations. BAAF has produced a leaflet, *Child from the past*, aimed at people who placed a child for adoption years ago, with information about the few steps they can take if they either want to encourage contact or want to avoid it.

SUPA·BOUNCE

❰❰ *I'm a mother who had a child nearly twenty years ago, alone. The baby's father was not already married – he could have married me if he had wanted to. I loved the father and I loved the baby all through the pregnancy and I loved her enough to give her away so that she could have a family. I would not have considered adoption if I had not thought that the adoptive parents had a lot more to offer than I. My cherished wish is to meet them, and to know how she is getting on.* ❱❱

❰❰ *When I finally decided that the best thing for the kids was not to go on trying to bring them up myself, I felt very guilty at first. People didn't want to know me. But the ups and downs of me going in and out of hospital had really messed their lives up and I wanted them to have some stability. I know now that I was right, not everybody else. Though I've missed them, they've had a much better chance than they would have had with me, as things turned out. I still think of them a lot, especially at Christmas and birthdays.* ❱❱

❰❰ *My thoughts for my daughter's adoptive parents have always been kind. I hope that I will meet them. I know it's a lot to ask, but hopefully as our society is changing, they will not see me as a threat. I can understand their attachment, the pride and love they have shared. The extra love I have cannot hurt. Even if the only mistake I made was having her adopted, I have had to accept so many things concerning her. I hope that they will accept that I exist and that I love her – but I love her enough not to try and tear her away from a family that has brought her up and still loves her.* ❱❱

❰❰ *Adopted children often don't seek out their birth parents as they feel they were given away or not wanted. This is far from the truth. I was 18, naive, vulnerable. I stayed at the mother and baby home until the birth of my daughter. We had choices, but looking back I was manipulated into giving up my child. 'Surely, if you love your daughter, you want the best for her – two loving parents who can give her a good and secure home etc.' So I was made to feel I had to give her up – as love my baby I did! But in all the time before the birth of my child and after not one person said to me, 'Have you thought of keeping your child?' Now, married with three further children, when each was born (and many more times besides) I have cried for the baby I should have kept. So my message to adoptees is: don't feel you were given up or unwanted. I wasn't the only young girl at that home and the majority were in the same boat.* ❱❱

*W*hen they reach a certain age, adoptive children in Britain have the right to see their original birth certificate. This means that they can find out the name of their birth mother (and sometimes father), if they don't already know it. They can also see their mother's address at that time (though very occasionally mothers gave a false address). With this information they can, if they choose, try to trace their birth parent(s) and perhaps make contact with them. Not all adopted children do, and certainly not all at the age of 17 or 18 do, but the numbers are growing.

Because recent changes in the law in England and Wales (not Scotland) were completely different from what had gone before (when adopted children *didn't* have the right to see their birth certificates), there are of course many birth parents from England and Wales who gave their child up for adoption as a baby expecting never

ABOUT TRACING BIRTH PARENTS

to have any future contact with them. So those children who were adopted before this law came into force have to have an interview with a counsellor (usually a social worker) before they can see their birth certificate. This is to give them a chance to think about the possible consequences of their seeing their certificate, including of course the consequences of finding their birth parent(s). And it's to help them understood a bit more about the possible feelings of their birth parent(s) now, so many years later. Children adopted more recently don't have to see a counsellor before getting their birth records.

How will you feel?
It's important for you to try not to see any interest your child might have in their birth parents as a threat to their relationship with you. Try to put yourself in their place. Wouldn't *you* be intrigued to know what your birth mother was like – what she looked like and how she felt about you? To find out a bit more about your father? It's a natural instinct, and much the best

way for you to deal with it is to be as positive as possible. You know more about your child than anyone, and you can help them. If you say something like 'When you're eighteen you can get your birth certificate and if you want to trace your birth parents I can help you', your child will involve you and won't feel embarrassed (as many do) or that they are being unfair to you. You won't run the risk, as many adopters have, of not being told that your adopted child is trying to trace their birth parents. But if, however positive you are, your child still feels uneasy and decides to leave you out or to discuss the search with someone else rather than you, try not to feel hurt. It can be a very difficult emotional time for your child. Having more than one set of parents is confusing. And remember, too, that the birth parent has had a real influence on the way your child has developed over the years, despite being absent, and your child has a right to find out more about that influence, if they choose. (The 'What is a parent?' box on page 21 might help.)

《 I was adopted in 1930 and felt there was little chance of tracing my family as so many records were destroyed during the war. I thought I would be content to just have my original birth certificate, but after my counselling session I became really interested in my birth family and decided to search . . . The experience of searching has taught me a lot. Firstly, I didn't think I would become emotionally involved: I didn't think I was that type. I found there were days when I was elated and had to play records really loudly to let off steam. Other days I had to work extra hard to hide bitter disappointment. I didn't feel I wanted to talk about it. Patience also was essential, and being an impatient person there were times when I was tempted to phone on the spur of the moment, and I'm ashamed to think of the distress this might have caused! 》

《 I have reached the point where I absolutely must know the truth about my origins. I did not feel this need until I had my first child. When I first saw my son I wept because he was the first living being I had ever seen to whom I was truly related. It was an overwhelming experience, a kind of total system-shock. I say this so you will know that this is not usually a teenage identity crisis. A large proportion of us in this position are in our 30s and 40s. I do not need a new mother, I've got a wonderful one of my own. I do not need a new family – mine is the best there is. I can never, however, expect to find the warm relation of my fantasies and I know it. What is it I want then? You who are not adopted cannot know what it is to be shut out of a family's history. 》

《 As many others who were adopted would agree, the need for truth and identity grows deeper with the years. That curiosity fluctuates between 'Well, I wasn't wanted then so why should now be any different?' and 'That's a chance I've got to take'. At various stages during my life I'd given very deep thought to the situation, particularly on my twenty-first birthday. Anyway, last year, with our four children all teenagers, I felt that my husband and I could at least spend a little of our spare time on the search. A little – that's a laugh – it took over our lives! My whole family were behind me in this venture and I feel sure I would not have managed without their support. My one big regret is not being able to confide in my adoptive mother. Over the years any questions from me resulted in tears and obvious distress, so I felt it would be unkind to say anything. Now of course I feel very guilty 》

Where can you get help?

If your child decides to apply for their birth certificate, the first thing to do is to write to:

The Registrar General
Adopted Children's Register
Titchfield
Fareham
Hants PO15 5RU
(for England & Wales) or to:

The General Registrar's Office
New Register House
Edinburgh
EH1 3Y1
(for Scotland).

Other sources of help are:
the adoption agency which placed your child
PPIAS (see page 28)
NORCAP (see page 28)
Post-Adoption Centre (see page 29)
BAAF (see page 29)
your local social services or social work department
telephone advice services (see page 29)

Parent to Parent Information on Adoption Services (PPIAS)

PPIAS is a national organisation for adoptive parents, their children and those hoping to adopt. There are about 100 branches scattered throughout the country and most of these hold meetings where a wide variety of topics related to adoption, including telling, can be discussed and there is the opportunity to meet people in similar circumstances. PPIAS members include many types of adoptive family, from those who have adopted healthy babies to those who have enlarged their family with one or more older or handicapped child. People intending to adopt can also join, as one of the best ways of finding out what adopting involves is to talk to people who've already done it.

Branches usually hold some family events such as summer picnics, Christmas parties, etc, where children can meet other adopted children.

The National Organisation for Counselling Adoptees and their Parents (NORCAP)

NORCAP is a support group that offers the opportunity to talk to people who have had similar experiences. There are many 'contact leaders' around the country.

NORCAP is campaigning for a *national register* to be established, containing medical and other non-identifying information on birth parents and adopted people. In the meantime it has started a simple contact register indexed by date and place of birth.

NORCAP aims to help and counsel:
adopted people who are thinking of searching for their birth parents – it will suggest ideas and viewpoints to be considered before making a decision which will have far-reaching consequences;
birth parents who either long for, or dread, a contact from the past – they can be put in touch

WHERE YOU CAN GET MORE HELP

From a child's point of view it's very comforting to have some friends who are adopted. It makes the whole thing seem more normal and less 'different', and it gives children the opportunity to share similar feelings and experiences. They enjoy going to the picnics and meeting their friends. Knowing other adoptive families with new children and babies arriving keeps the subject near the surface and discussable. PPIAS produce a regular newsletter full of fascinating experiences of adopters and adopted people. It's worth joining just to read this.

Parent to Parent Information on Adoption Services is at:
Lower Boddington
Daventry
Northants
NN11 6YB.

telephone (0327) 60295

with others in the same position;
adoptive parents whose lives will be affected by any search their adopted children may start – it offers reassurance that they are only trying to find out more about themselves, and can provide information on ways of answering their child's questions.

NORCAP encourages the use of intermediaries in making any contact.

Members receive a quarterly newsletter and can buy other publications.

NORCAP is at:
3 New High Street
Headington
Oxford
OX3 7AJ.

telephone (0865) 750554

Post-Adoption Centre (PAC)

PAC provides a service for adoptive families, adopted people and birth parents whose children were adopted. The Centre offers counselling, preferably in person, but also on the telephone or by correspondence, for individuals and families. It also organises events which focus on matters related to adoption, and provides the opportunity for people to meet in common interest groups.

The Centre was established in recognition of the fact that adoption is a process which may raise new issues, for any of the participants, at different stages of life. It offers free professional advice, in a neutral setting, where the experience of adoption is understood and neither denied nor over-emphasised.

It is often not easy for parents to talk to a child about adoption, whether the child's background is straightforward or complex. The Centre arranges a periodic programme of workshops to help parents explore some of the issues involved in communicating with children about adoption and to consider new ideas and approaches.

The Post-Adoption Centre is at:
Gregory House
48 Mecklenburgh Square
London WC1N 2NU.

telephone (01) 833 2314/5

British Agencies for Adopting & Fostering (BAAF)

BAAF is a registered charity and professional association for all those working in the child care field. BAAF's work includes:

giving advice and information to members of the public on aspects of adoption, fostering and child care issues;

publishing a wide range of books, training packs and leaflets as well as a quarterly journal on adoption, fostering and child care issues;

providing training and consultation services to social workers and other professionals to help them improve the quality of medical, legal and social work services to children and families;

giving evidence to government committees on subjects concerning children and families;

responding to consultative documents on changes is legislation and regulations affecting children in or at risk of coming into care;

and helping to find new families for children through the BAAF Exchange Service, 'Be My Parent' and 'Find a Family'.

More information about BAAF (including addresses of regional offices) can be obtained from: BAAF
11 Southwark Street
London SE1 1RQ.

telephone (01) 407 8800

Telephone advice services

Numbers	Days	Times	Organisation
London (01) 668 2181/4	Every weekday	9.00–5.30	Catholic Children's Society
Woking (048 62) 69229	Tuesdays	9.30–4.30	National Children's Home
London (01) 551 0011	Wednesdays	12.30–4.30	Dr Barnardo's
Glasgow (041) 339 0772	Wednesdays	2.00–5.00 6.30–9.00	Scottish Adoption Advice Service
Edinburgh (031) 225 3666	Every weekday	9.00–5.00	Family Care
Dublin (0001) 960042	Tuesdays	2.00–6.00	Dr Barnardo's
Oxford (0865) 750554	Monday Wednesday Friday	10.00–4.00	NORCAP

Books for adopted children

Althea **Jane is adopted** Souvenir Press, 1980
The hows and whys of adoption are simply outlined in this illustrated story book suitable for children up to seven or eight.

Averill E **Jenny and the cat club** Collins, 1976
A stray cat is 'adopted' by a sympathetic master. She has to learn to fit into a new neighbourhood. Jenny persuades her owner to adopt two brothers but things do not work out too well. Jealousy grows as they begin to take over all her favourite toys and corners. A family crisis follows but it all works out in the end.

Bond M **Here comes Thursday** Puffin, 1966
In the first two chapters of this book Thursday, who was brought up in the 'home for waif-mice and stray-mice' finds a new meaning to life when he is accepted as a member of a family of shopkeeper mice.

USEFUL BOOKS

Bond M **The Paddington books** Collins
These books are well known to most children but remember that Paddington has to get used to living in a family for the first time. He brought with him from Peru his scrapbook, a photo of his Aunt Lucy and little else. He settles down in his new home despite many traumatic experiences but often thinks back to his past.

Bunin, C and S **Is that your sister?** Pantheon Books, 1976
Slightly dated, this is a sympathetically written true story in the words of a six-year-old black girl, Catherine, who was adopted into a white American family. The time of adoption of a younger girl, Carla, is also told. They are photographed throughout.

Edwards D and Dinan C **Robert goes to fetch a sister** Methuen, 1986
A story of transracial adoption, for young children of three to seven. Robert, adopted as a baby, listens again to his own story and goes with his parents to collect a new baby.

Frendberg J and Geiss T **Susan and Gordon adopt a baby** Random House, 1986
Based on the American TV series 'Sesame Street', this is the story of black parents who adopt a baby, aided (or hampered) by the puppet 'Big Bird'. It can be used to help explain adoption to a young (four to seven year old) child.

Lapsley S **I am adopted** The Bodley Head, 1982
Delightful bed-time story for very small children and beautifully illustrated by Michael Charlton, this describes the life at home of Charles and Sophie. Charles says that they are adopted and that 'adoption means belonging'.

Livingston C **Why was I adopted?** Angus & Robertson, 1981
This book is great fun. It provides clear information for the enquiring child in a lively and humorous way. Its main lack is that there are no black children or adults illustrated. It is suitable for five to ten year olds.

McAfee A and Browne A **The visitors who came to stay** Hamish Hamilton, 1984
Kate lives alone with her dad. Life changes when Mary and her son Sean become regular visitors. An unusual and amusing book with remarkable illustrations.

Olsen MV **The fur children** Collins, 1981
A pregnant cat is taken in by a sympathetic family. The kittens are born, grow up and explore until they are all adopted by different families and go to live in their new homes. Beautifully illustrated.

Snell N **Sam's new dad** Hamish Hamilton, 1983
An agreeable little book for very young children. Sam's parents are separated. He lives with his mother and sees his father most weekends. His mother marries Bill and Sam likes this: 'He would always love his own dad, but now he would have someone to play with all the time'.

Snell N **Steve is adopted** Hamish Hamilton, 1985
Steve is a little black boy adopted into a white family. He feels 'It's nice to feel wanted'. This

story book could be used with small children asking about adoption and being black or brown in a white family. (He is described in the book as being brown.)

Wright B **My new Mum and me** Blackwell Raintree, 1982
This is a touching story of a young girl coming to terms with the death of her mother and life with her new step-mother. It could be used with children of all ages who have to deal with grief and loss, step-parents and step-parent adoption.

Teenage novels

Garfield L **The sound of coaches** Penguin Books, 1977
Conflicts of loyalty experienced by a boy adopted by a coachman and his wife: he seeks and finds the truth about his first parents. (Suitable for older children and adults considering seeking birth records.)

Holm A **I am David** Penguin Books, 1969
A boy's escape from a prison camp and his search for his mother and his identity.

Lowry L **Find a stranger, say goodbye** Viking Kestrel Books, 1980
The story of an adopted girl's search for her birth mother. Everything is going well in her present family but she needs to know her background. She carries out her search in a responsible way and the feelings it stirs up are realistic. Eventually she finds her birth mother and returns to her adoptive family who she discovers to be her 'real' parents.

Nerlove E **Who is David?** Child Welfare League of America, Inc, 1985
An involving story that should capture the attention of many adopted adolescents, especially boys. David struggles with his curiosity about his original parents, in a happy adoptive home. His emerging friendship with Diana is sensitively described.

Noel D **Five to seven: the story of a 1920s childhood** Robin Clark, 1980
A small girl copes with the terrors of life caused by unpredictable adults, and separation from the key figure in her life.

Pearce P **The way to sattin shore** Viking Kestrel, 1983
Kate's family refuse to tell her about her dead father. They do not understand that until she finds out the truth about her father she cannot cope with living in the present.

Books on 'the facts of life'

Kaufman J **All about us** Hamlyn, 1976
An excellent book which covers reproduction, the functioning of the body and how to look after it. Emphasises the importance of senses.

Rayner C **The body book** Pan Books, 1978
A delightfully written and illustrated book, this deals with all the difficult subjects like where babies come from and what death is about in an interesting and sympathetic way. It should be useful with many an adopted child's questions.

Books for adoptive parents

Adopting a child: a guide for people interested in adoption BAAF, 1986
Essential reading for anyone who is considering adopting a child and very useful for existing adoptive parents, this down-to-earth guide gives clear and up-to-date information on all stages of the adoption process. It includes names and addresses of adoption and fostering agencies throughout the country, with maps showing their location, and details of other organisations concerned with adoption.

Austin J (ed) **Adoption. The inside story** Barn Owl Books, 1985
Written by adoptive parents, this book contains real-life stories covering the pleasures and pains of adoption today, including a chapter 'Telling: sharing the past'. The experiences of parents who have evolved successful ways of describing their children's pasts provide ideas and encouragement.

continued overleaf

Jones M **Everything you need to know about adoption** Sheldon House (SPCK), 1987
A very useful guide to adoption with plenty of quotations from people who've 'done it'. Includes material on transracial and inter-country adoption.

Rowe J **Yours by choice. A guide for adoptive parents** Routledge Kegan Paul, 1982
This sympathetically written guide for parents includes an excellent chapter on explaining adoption. Jane Rowe describes the hows and whys of being clear and straightforward about the past.

Ryan T and Walker R **Making life story books** BAAF, 1985
An invaluable guide to the innovative and imaginative techniques now available to help children come to terms with their painful pasts. It outlines the background theory and offers games and projects like family trees, maps and life graphs that aid the healing process. Illustrated with drawings and photographs.

BAAF leaflets

If you are adopted
Answers to some of the questions adopted children ask, aimed at the children themselves. Includes information on tracing birth parents. Illustrated.

Talking about origins
An outline of adopted children's need to be told about adoption and the law on access to birth certificates.

See also leaflets mentioned on pages 21 and 25.

For further reading

For those parents who want to read further and explore psychological and other evidence which shows the importance of openness about adoption, the following will provide a good starting point:

Bower T **The perceptual world of the child** Fontana Open Books ('The developing child' series), 1977

Erikson E H **Childhood & society** Triad/Paladin, 1977

Kirk H D **Shared fate: a theory of adoption and mental health** Collier Macmillan, 1964

Kirk H D **Adoptive Kinship** Butterworth, 1982

Piaget J **The child's conception of the world** Paladin, 1973

Triseliotis J **In search of origins** Routledge Kegan Paul, 1973

Triseliotis J (ed) **New developments in foster care and adoption** Routledge Kegan Paul, 1980

Articles regularly appear in the BAAF quarterly journal **Adoption & Fostering** which may be of interest to adoptive parents. For subscription details, contact BAAF.